A
RETIRING
PRIEST

A
RETIRING
PRIEST

From There To Here

PETER WALKER

A record of this publication is available from the British Library.

ISBN 978-1-910027-40-0

Typesetting by Wordzworth Ltd
www.wordzworth.com

Cover design by Titanium Design Ltd
www.titaniumdesign.co.uk

Cover image: bridge at Builth Wells, Wales,
by kind permission of Visit Wales, Welsh Government

**LOCAL
LEGEND**   Published by Local Legend
www.local-legend.co.uk

The Author

Peter Walker is a teacher, priest and poet. His last collection *The House of Being* won the national Local Legend Spiritual Writing Competition in 2018.

After graduating in French and Philosophy, he taught languages for many years while at the same time training for the priesthood. It was the birth of his daughter that brought him an intense, personal experience of sacred, numinous love leading to his ordination in the Church of England. He is now retired – although, of course, priests never truly retire, they simply move from active ministry to a more informal role.

Peter's new work reflects in particular his experience as a priest in Wales and his interest in Celtic spirituality, whilst it is also deeply in tune with and influenced by the natural world. Yet he is nonetheless down-to-earth, loving "red wine and strong coffee, the vibrancy of the inner city and the deserted shoreline at dawn, the music of Muddy Waters and of Vaughan Williams."

He is married to Susie, with whom he has a daughter and a grandson.

Previous Publications

Penmon Point   ISBN 978-1847713698 (2011)
Old Men in Jeans   ISBN 978-1847714343 (2012)
Listening to Zappa   ISBN 978-1847717030 (2013)
A Pocketful of Myrrh ISBN 978-1784611415 (2015)
Published by Y Lolfa, Tal-y-bont, Ceredigion, Mid-Wales

The House of Being   ISBN 978-1-910027-26-4 (2018)
Winner of the national Local Legend Spiritual Writing Competition 2018

This Book

There are times in everyone's journey of life when new paths open up to us. Some of these are chosen or arrive unexpectedly, whilst some are inevitable. Each one, however, presents us with opportunities to learn and to grow, in consciousness and in spirit.

When Peter Walker retired from Church ministry there was inevitably some sense of loss, especially of the close relationship he'd had with his community and of the sacred rituals he felt privileged to conduct. Yet he could now devote more time to his own growing family and to a new, different community of diverse interests.

This new collection of poems therefore naturally falls into two distinct parts, charting the journey from 'There' to 'Here' as the path unfolds to a different way of life and calling. The first part reflects on important theological issues and priestly concerns that still linger in the mind, whilst the second part is more personal and observant of everyday life and nature, no less sacred.

In their entirety, all of these poems, says Peter, "deal with our human brokenness, our sense of mortality and our deep human need for love, community and our search for spiritual truths."

Acknowledgements

We are grateful to Y Lolfa for permission to republish *St Asaph Pilgrimage*, which first appeared in their anthology *Travelling With the Saints*.

Contents

From There To Here   1

I   **FROM THERE...**   **3**

St Asaph Pilgrimage   4

Autumn At Noddfa   5

Tuesday   6

Psalm CLI   7

Substitute   8

Remembrance Day   10

The Glorious Dead   11

Whispering All Together   12

Chi-Zen   13

Llanrhos Churchyard   14

Maelgwn   15

Invisible   16

The Dark Van   17

Once   18

Y Pethau Bychain   19

The Morning Mist   20

Quentin Said...   21

The Chaplain   22

Someone Else's Sermon (Ascension Day)   23

No-One Will Write My Biography   24

A Meet of Poets   26

II   ...TO HERE   **27**

Do You Remember Me?   28

The Bridge at Queensferry   29

Trains   30

Ink   32

The Traveller   33

Tale of a Shropshire Lad   34

S.B.   35

Lagan   36

Gulls   37

The Sheep on the Dunes   38

Sand   39

Shower   40

Coronation Garden   41

Thin Ice   42

Brooklands Avenue   43

Max   44

Rimrose

    (i) Dawn   45

    (ii) May   45

    (iii) The Rowan Tree   46

    (iv) Jet Trails In September   47

    (v) First Frost   47

    (vi) November   48

    (vii) Christmas Day   48

From There To Here

there are other places
and
there are other times
but I am here
by fate and inclination

what was
is not
and has been mined for approbation
and my own delight
and is a ripple in the sand

what is
will be
but darkly seen
we do not fill the cup
but wait for its filling DV

not there
but here
where time slides helter-skelter
and you seek to grab a hand
for safety or for comfort or to show you care

not here
but ultimately there
but darkly seen
we merely glimpse the way
and wait for guiding DV

there are other places
and
there are other times
but I am here
by fate and inclination

1

I.

FROM THERE...

St Michael and All Angels church, Llandudno Junction, Wales

St Asaph Pilgrimage

I take the name of psalm-bringer
from monks' house to saints' rest
ascending to the holy places
across the storms of mountains
and the high hill seas

with awe before the void
or the phenomenology of our emotions
anger at my own complicity in the world's woes
shame at my secret lives
joy in the simplicity of little things
in the woodwind cuckoo and the blackbird flute
the intermingling emulsion of our genes

and so we make a pilgrimage of words
into the inner workings of our vocabulary
where we stand in silence
before the dyslexic letters of our perception
seeking to make sense with the grammar of our morality
and thus construct a narrative of grace
for our journey's end

yet however far we travel we are drawn into ourselves
to echoes
souls
apophasis
darkness
light

such is the emptiness we seek
to find it filled with possibility

St Asaph was the first bishop of the Diocese of St Asaph, taking his name
from the author of many Old Testament psalms.

Autumn At Noddfa

in these short autumn days
the leaves do not stay long in the tall trees
as the brushed drum of the wind sweeps them away
with a skirl at the window pane

the bare branches are thin and brittle as bones
beneath the skin of sky
they point the way to winter and its long sunset
spilling its purple along the western fringe

yet this too will fade and soften
for beneath the calloused carapace of earth
the fragile seed is drawing warmth into itself
and learning how to be what it might be

so I wait for the wind to touch my face
and beneath this pale flesh
there is yet something which cannot be ignored
that hints at light and fire

*Noddfa is Welsh for 'refuge', a place for retreats, refreshment and group
events near Penmaenmawr in North Wales.*

Tuesday

salvation comes on Tuesday
whatever that may mean
for the word itself is suspect
and pregnant with a gross of definitions

let me bathe in mystery
and wallow in the unexplained
with the murky mud of almost-glimpsed
and a cloud of Prinknash incense
swirling

for metaphysics is the art of the beyond
imagining the unimaginable into life
as music takes its form in the composer's head
and words between lovers are left unsaid

Psalm CLI

when I have been lost and broken
you have sought me out

when I have betrayed myself and others
you have kept faith with me

when I have searched and not found
you have been my compass

when I have turned my back on those in pain
you have forgiven my lack of compassion

when I have faced the pain of the world
you have shed tears with me

when I have held the hand of the fearful
you have been my shield

when I have laughed and sung with joy
you have smiled at my delight

when I have loved deeply
so deeply
you have rejoiced with me

Substitute

with rictus certainty
and arms held high
to blot my silent prayers
they tell me this...

the thorn-crowned butterfly
snatched in beauteous flight
is pinned within the sanctuary
with wings stretched wide

the naturalist has caught his prize
and thus releases marbled white
and tortoiseshell
orange-tip
fritillary and emperor
who now are freed
to pay their homage at the shrine
of stapled feather-dust
but fail to bow
ignore the sacrifice

then fear the entomologist
who
in fit of pique
will vent his wrath
on flitting fearful man-moth
and burn his wings in candle-flame

my lepidopterist
if truth be known
keeps chrysalis guarded tight
and marvels at the womb-wet wing
calls us toward warm tropic heart
and breeds in us the genes
of love
that flower in us the pain
of squirming thorax
that we ourselves have pinned
onto the tree

Remembrance Day

remembrance(d) sky

princessed clouds of candied cotton

turquoise wash
bright as a six-year old's vision
with a thick red brush stirred to unbristled nothing
in a deep pit of green and blue

a Somme sky

a Helmand sky

a blackbird-whistled sky for corpse rising

and then
old medalled men
whose clinking tin and Morse-tap canes
tick out their "Why, again?"

The Glorious Dead

they never take to drink or play away
beat their children or their wives
go bankrupt
become revisionist in their politics
(yet remain firm and absolute in their convictions)
lose their faith or waver from the creeds and facts
look back with fondness on a world no longer there
vanished like a magician's silver coin
never catch a cancer or the pox
never see their child in pain

and yet their cold-white faces
(chiselled marble on a plinth)
would melt
if they could take the place
of the bent and crippled
whose bony fingers tap their temple
to invoke a story lost in time
and whose pale opaque eyes
are filled with memory and joy

Whispering All Together

we start a rumour of love
and people talk of naïve innocence

in a world of nails and dogma
our lambs' tongues will be plucked by crows
as we stand
drifted in snow
and we will retch to bleat out our desires

yet still trees are climbed
and bloodied hands pressed
to give the benediction of forgiveness

such whispering
may yet change the world

Chi-Zen

the way cannot be told...

God is love
three-in-one and one-in-three
like Joshu's dog
(does a dog have a soul?
and the reply came "Do you have a soul?")

it is only in the soaring notes
that the words begin to have sense
because they do not matter except for their inarticulate...
and if I lived an if then this would be a butterfly-winged world
with alien beings
and another me

do you understand...
these are what we ponder when reason ties in knots
inch time foot gem

Jesus had a Buddha soul
Buddha had a Jesus soul

I cannot tell the way
the way cannot be told...
and yet this does not mean there is not a way

the way cannot be told...

Llanrhos Churchyard

the full moon is gnawed by a bite of cloud
as in the east
beneath the watch of Venus
there is the slow leak of sun between the pines

the wreaths have gone now
the petals dry and cracked and blown away
replaced by solar bulbs of red and green
the little lights that mark the space that scars
as if we cannot grasp the concept of eternity
unless it is mapped out by stars

yet even they will fade in time

a wandering stray snuffles
nuzzles
and digs for old bones
and pricks her ears as she senses a presence
perhaps

Maelgwn

when Maelgwn stooped
yellow-eyed
he saw the maidens riding on the crests of waves

and in that very time
when wolf-hound and wolf are indistinguishable
the plague-maidens rode in
with hair as silver as the salted spray
and gowns like the translucent scales of the sea-bass

and with his eye he caught
the slow pornography of his own death
and knelt to breathe his last half-believed prayer
at the spot where his bones still lie today
they say

Maelgwn Gwynedd was the sixth century king of Gwynedd whose stronghold was Deganwy Castle. He was reputedly struck down by the 'yellow plague' in his church at Llanrhos and legend says he is buried within its confines.

Invisible

("The poet is the priest of the invisible." Wallace Stevens)

the priest is the poet of the invisible

writing names in water
until it is sticky with sin

conjuring bread and wine
into flesh and blood
we are cannibals of the infinite

holding the butterfly of hope
in an open hand
and a petal of rose-red redemption in the other

seeking to magic what salvation means
in a fractal
of broken hearts

The Dark Van

there is a dark van
that cruises summer streets
driven by men in black suits and ties

whether in sun-flecked mornings
with dappled shadows and birdsong
breeze-blown cool blue sky
or
bright noon of amber glare
with honey-humming bees
on mossy shaded walls

the black windows of the van
oblivious and unblinking
shielding from view
the still still-cooling heart
and silted veins

a slow chemical procession

summer bleeds
to brown leaf
and icy snapping twigs

Once

(For Dilwyn, brother priest.)

once have I met God
like Isaiah
not behind the dark-stained oak
or beneath a table caparisoned in green or white
but as I rose high on Mynydd Llandygai
with a lake of pale white mist at my feet
that stretched
to Llanberis and beyond
while birds played fanfares to the dawn
crisp and blue and full of hope

twice have I met God
not in rage and rant and pettiness
not in purple
but in broken bodies in wards of pain
with the slow breath of their diminishing
and the way that Glory showed in their passion
then I saw the truth of wafer and of wine
that our deep frailty is a glimpse of the divine

three times have I met God
not in triumph or in pleasure
or in words of faith
but in my own thin flesh
that grows transparent with the rub of life
and lets me read eternity on the braille of my skin
and like Isaiah
feel the brush of a passing cloak

Y Pethau Bychain

to wait
by the bed of one who waits

to hold the hand
of one who longs for warmth

to sit
by one who sits in silence wondering

to look into the eyes
of one who is lost and yearns to be seen

to listen
to the burdens of another's soul

to speak
to one who strains to hear of comfort

to point
to the aching heart of the One who loves

"Gwnewch y pethau bychain." (Do the little things.) This was reputedly said by Dewi Sant (Saint David) to his followers shortly before his death. The words continue to be a key phrase in ministry.

The Morning Mist

the morning mist
that floated in
like a vast white sail
and enveloped
wave and shore
and the damp spiked grass
now drapes the wooded slopes
like the dribbled rags of November fires
and hides the top of Cadair
from the valley's eye

Quentin Said...

...there's a poem in that
...tall twisted tales of purple and the guile of women
...the sown seed that sprouts sixty-fold or more
...rifts and rumours measuring maturity
...massaging numbers lest we are seen to fail

the little things
the searching out the lost
the tears
standing in the breach with arms outstretched
an icon of loss or victory
we know not which

for eternity is confused
unclear
a tune by Hindemith

The Chaplain

they talk with that same voice of authority
that same accent
undefined and indefinable
except to say

I have learned to be rootless

forgetting
that life is sustained
by that which grows beneath the soil

Someone Else's Sermon
(Ascension Day)

and with the efflorescence
came sin
and more sin
John Calvin
(three times)
Karl Barth and even
(goodness knows from where)
the blessed John Henry Newman
(covering all the bases)

and all of this
above the sleeping
nodding heads
an ascension of ideas
that left us rooted
Earth-bound
when we might have soared with wonder
and been drawn to live
that risen life

No-One Will Write My Biography

no-one will write my biography

shallow pool
where shrimp dart
transparent
but for bead-black eye and flicking feeler
where anemone tucks in pulsing digits
lest the frying sun
turn them to toasted brittle twigs
where the pink-orange pimple starfish
slow as tortoise
beguiled by wavelet lap and ripple
is now stiff and dry
leathern as beef jerky
pale as bone
which will be consumed by cool-cruel tide

and yet

the ink spilt in the womb
creates an image that thinks my thoughts
at the very moment of their thinking
but is now making mirrors of its own

and yet

some will recall
the joke and gesture
rhyme and reason
accent and applause
failure and success
reality and dream

sometimes
in love's embrace
this is enough

sometimes
on the icy
wind-blown scree
a cold
cold tear will leak

A Meet of Poets

sometimes we skirt around each other
warily
like dogs sniffing for snarls
too alike in our genes to leave the pack
yet too dissimilar in form
to band together and hunt the quarry

for we are leashed to our own mistress
and fearful
to leave her side
for in her eyes only are we made
and we respond to her voice as it calls
across the wastes of time and space
and when she pats us we bristle with pride

the world does not comprehend such loyalty

II.

...TO HERE

Do You Remember Me?

do you remember

that sullen child
petulant
self-absorbed
who spurned the dream of spires
the drinker-in of life
intoxicated by one small cup
hiding loss and pain and failure
re-invented by the universe
and finding God and love
in equal measure

do you remember

sometimes I do not remember myself

The Bridge at Queensferry

old coat landscape soft as leather
no thought of
mill or tannery
abattoir or slum
we slough off
our snakeskin yesterday
and leave it drying in the sun

but
beneath the pulse of rise and fall
unnoticed heartbeat of the thrumming tyres
there is the scalpel scar that lets the warm blood flow
and from this flow
we fill the vials of our todays
unsure of our inheritance
and fail to recognise
the genes
that make us who we are

Trains

I travelled by train
with its clackety-clack and its clackety-clack
when I was three with my parents
for a week in a caravan in Kinmel Bay
and all I can remember is the hot
hot sand
that burned my shins
and the turquoise sea that shone with stars

I travelled by train
with its clackety-clack and its clackety-clack
when I was fourteen with a mate to Butlin's
we lied about our age
and got drunk on warm Watney's Red Barrel
I danced to the Temptations in my houndstooth hipster slacks
and we tried to pick up girls
Deana and Sharon
Sandra and Marguerite

I travelled by train
with its clackety-clack and its clackety-clack
when I was seventeen to a different city and a different life
its mystery and yearning
days of learning
and nights of smokey lust and
sometimes
love

I travelled by train
with its clackety-clack and its clackety-clack
when I was twenty
back from the warm easy south
and when I got near home
I went into the corridor and let down the window
on its wide leather strap
and smelled the hot metal and the burning coal
saw the sparks of the welders and the factory flames
the dirty cut water heavy with barges
and the sparse grass by the brickworks
and further on
the rear of my grandfather's house
with its neat clipped lawn
the white linen on the washing line

and I swear I could smell the roses
that opened their delicate hearts for me

Ink

my grandmother warned me
never to get a tattoo

in my childhood
as I rode my tricycle through the park
she would tut
at the blue-inked forearms of the navvies in the road
as they swung their picks
or lifted heaving mugs of tea

and later she would scoff
at ageing sun-bleached mothers
whose heavy breasts would stretch their tee-shirts
to reveal a blood-red rose
or a once-fashionable name

and in the summer heat
her one concession
was to push the sleeves of her snow-white cardigan
up to her elbow and reveal
the pastel numbers on her wrist

The Traveller

if I were a trav'ller
I would steal your heart away
to make sure that you loved me
every night and every day

if I were a Romany
I'd wander all this land
and when I came back home again
I'd ask you for your hand

if I were a tinker
I would make a ring of gold
to show you that my love for you
is strong and brave and bold

if I were a hobo
I would search this world in vain
looking for the love I lost
that will not come again

and so I am a trav'ller
who will tell your future true
of love and loss and sadness
for you know I am like you

for all of us are travellers
and we have a traveller's soul
and all of us are looking
for the love that makes us whole

Tale of a Shropshire Lad

when I sat by the Severn
my love sat by my side
we were but one-and-twenty
and she swore to be my bride

but I was young and foolish
when I gave my heart away
for she chose rings and velvet gowns
and factory men who'd pay

so now beside the Severn
as I watch the trout that leap
I think of all those kisses
and the love I could not keep

the waters roll to Coalport
with the memories I hide
and bear them to the rolling sea
and cast them on the tide

so now beside the Severn
with my three score years and ten
I think about the love I lost
and wish her back again

S.B.

the dream
is the eternal dream
until we wake

the hope
is the unending hope
until it dies

the plans
are morning light
until the dark

the future
is a bridge of possibilities
until the tightrope snap
of our mortality

we wake
we sleep
and in-between
we trust there is the warmth
to heal cold hearts
and tempt them back to love

Lagan

the downed trunk
beached in waves of grass
is bleached bone-white
like a bagged corpse
(I surmise)
insect-picked and pecked

and yet
the land is dressed in green
sewn with the beat of wings
and tacked in time with the sweet bloom of life
that leaks from each leaf's sticky pore

and between these two
the hum of engines
as the land shakes with ferry swirl and diesel spume
and the Lagan makes its own slow way
towards the dock
and shows us that
sometimes
we need to cross the sea
to feel that we are home

a pilgrim journey
to the place we left nigh on a lifetime ago
for we are creatures of our own imagining
and none the less for that

M.S. Stena Lagan is one of the ferries on the route between Birkenhead and Belfast.

Gulls

the lost souls of the gulls
sing out above harp music

their throats still
as they take to wing
a flurry of snow
swirling around
the deep drift of shingle

The Sheep on the Dunes

the sheep on the dunes
follow the well-worn path
and move in file
calm
irascible
wool heavy with dew

some turn aside
to bite low on luscious tufts
but keep a wary eye on those ahead
others group in twos or threes
for solidarity
and dash to join the flock
that makes its way
between the winding shore
and the straightened steel
heading home
ever-hungry for the light

Sand

in these warm March days
I saw the children digging on the beach at Blundellsands
and remembered...

...wind-whipped at Abermaw
cold wet shins speckled with sand dust
we tapped the upturned bucket six times
a tower at each corner like Harlech
and two for the gatehouse
with its portcullis of driftwood sticks
the walls made high with
all the refuse from the moat
as deep as our small arms could make them

and then we watched the tide
sidle its way with sly precision
to fill our trench with murky sea and laughter
and each tower slowly tumbled down
and the portcullis twigs were carried God knows where
separate and alone

and the next day as the tide ebbed back again
there was just a dim rise
to show where we had been upon the sand

Shower

on Crosby Street South
the late spring rain took us by surprise
and fell in drops as big as an old penny

the old man in shorts and trainers
stranded by the bollard
turned to face the traffic
his Jesus and Mary Chain tee-shirt
shower-damp but proud
a uniform of times before the storm

Coronation Garden

in Coronation Garden
our steps are marked by
each bench that bears a name

in the fading letters
bleached by salt and rain
we find some semblance of eternity

yet here the hawthorn and the elderflower
the beech tree spreads its palms
the early dew is cold upon the heel
and wakes the green
and a white rose is teased
to spread its petals in the morning sun

Thin Ice

we almost danced
but the syncopated beat of the music
left us toe-tied
and stumbling for steps

we almost swam
but the hidden depth beneath
left us wondering
and shivering for breath

we almost skated
but the cracked mirror under our feet
left us shimmering
and scurrying for the shore

Brooklands Avenue

there is a dead rat in the gutter in Brooklands Avenue
as stiff and flat as card
ironed by Joe's Toyota as he eases off the kerb
the bright crimson veins are stretched and bright
like strawberry-flavoured sugar laces
ignored by scavenging magpies

later
washed by rain
they are blue-white chitterlings

later still
the muddied fur is frozen grey with a hard morning frost
and kicked skimming across the road by Tommy
on his way to school
an early lesson in his study of ecology

Max

(For Louise.)

I counted fingers and toes
"Is she alright?" I asked
the nurse in the delivery room said
"Yes
she's perfect"
and you were

and as I held you
(still wet from birth fluids)
you held the tip of my little finger
in your clenched palm
and this fallen
broken world
was itself become perfect
in that one sweet moment
and now you know that moment for yourself

the trick is
we need to hold that finger-tip of perfection
tight within our clenched palms
and not let go

Rimrose

(Rimrose Valley is a country park in Sefton, Merseyside.)

(i) Dawn

hawk hovers
as still as the full moon
wings as beating clouds
holding...
holding...
and then gone
swoop and rise
sculling the air
then back to the feeding lair
in the stunted oak

swifts gather as a storm
swirl and pirouette
dancers on the ice of air
to stake their claim
to the hawk space
in the rising light

(ii) May

despite these warm Spring days
there was a frost this morning
early
the lace edging
crisp and white beneath the toes
masking the dusty weariness
of the dried and rain-starved blades beneath
the weather vane on St Mary's leans
perilous
it no longer tells how the wind comes and goes
but stands above a hollow that we seek to fill

(iii) The Rowan Tree

in these late August mornings
the mist is slow to rise above the damp grass
in the low field by the valley stream
yet the rowan is flush with hands of scarlet joy
and its dropped tears ache with longing
they presage change
and the full swelling of the inner eye

the early windfalls from the wild-grown sparseness
of the Worcesters and the Bramleys and the mint-fresh Coxes
(hard as billiards and pale as fresh limes)
foretell the coming ripeness of the harvest months
and the growth that comes from my spasmodic nurture
(haphazard
and yet full of the need to bring to crop)

all o'erseen by the squad of rowans
standing guard
my Aquarian Celtic watchmen
protecting the innate seed and calling it to fruit

(iv) Jet Trails In September

pristine white chalk line
ruled and pencil-thin
against the powdered blue
higher than the fading feather
and the wisps of jagged mackerel skin beneath

arrivals and departures on the stage of sky

in the dew-cool morning
the geese and mallards and the ivory swans
throatily announce their Vulcan flight
in quick succession
one two three
calling as they gather

arrivals and departures on the stage of sky

(v) First Frost

in late October
as time turns back
to warm us by the fire of our memories
the new early light
shows each blade of grass soldered with cold
and yesterday's slipshod path is firm and crisp
unmarked by my passing
save for the dust of ice filings
gathered on my boots

(vi) November

I am standing in Rimrose facing east
and the dawn is red on the underclouds

the far cumulus casts sparse nets of grey rain
against the blue

the sun rises
gold behind the knuckles of the bare trees

until
visible in all its glory
it becomes impossible to look on

but this one glance
will satisfy until the spring

(vii) Christmas Day

the crooked finger of the old moon
telling of regret and reprobation
is no more

the birds in flight are calling out good news
the muddied ground is drying
firm

as the sky reddens with the rising sun
there are lights in children's rooms
excited by the gifts brought by the dawn

tonight there will be a beckoning
the invitation of the new moon
arched
like an angel's wing

If you have enjoyed this book...

Local Legend is committed to publishing the very best spiritual writing, both fiction and non-fiction. You might also enjoy:

THE HOUSE OF BEING
Peter Walker (ISBN 978-1-910027-26-4)

Acutely observed verse by a master of his craft, showing us the mind, the body and the soul of what it is to be human in this glorious natural world. A linguist and a priest, the author takes us deep beneath the surface of life and writes with sensitivity, compassion and, often, with searing wit and self-deprecation. This is a collection the reader will return to again and again.

A winner of our national *Spiritual Writing Competition*.

A MESSAGE FROM SOURCE
Grace Gabriella Puskas (ISBN 978-1-910027-00-4)

Beautiful and inspiring poetry of the Spirit that reaches deep within the consciousness, awakening the reader to higher states of awareness, spiritual connection and love. The author, in familiar and thoughtful language, explores the power of meditation, the nature of the universe and of time, our place within the environment and who we truly are as creative beings of light and sound.

Past winner of the Local Legend national
Spiritual Writing Competition.

GHOSTS OF THE NHS
Glynis Amy Allen (ISBN 978-1-910027-34-9)

It is rare to find an account of interaction with the spirit world that is so wonderfully down-to-earth! The author simply gives us one extraordinary true story after another, as entertaining as they are evidential. Glynis, an hereditary medium, worked for thirty years as a senior hospital nurse in the National Health Service, mostly in A&E wards. Almost on a daily basis, she would see patients' souls leave their bodies escorted by spirit relatives or find herself working alongside spirit doctors – not to mention the Grey Lady, a frequent ethereal visitor! A unique contribution to our understanding of life, this book was an immediate bestseller.

AURA CHILD
A I Kaymen (ISBN 978-1-907203-71-8)

One of the most astonishing books ever written, telling the true story of a genuine Indigo child. Genevieve grew up in a normal London family but from an early age realised that she had very special spiritual and psychic gifts. She saw the energy fields around living things, read people's thoughts and even found herself slipping through time and able to converse with the spirits of those who had lived in her neighbourhood. This is an uplifting and inspiring book for what it tells us about the nature of our minds.

A SINGLE PETAL
Oliver Eade (ISBN 978-1-907203-42-8)

Winner of the first national Local Legend *Spiritual Writing Competition*, this page-turner is a novel of murder, politics and passion set in ancient China. Yet its themes of loyalty, commitment and deep personal love are every bit as relevant for us today as they were in past times. The author is an expert on Chinese culture and history, and his debut adult novel deserves to become a classic.

"An intriguing mystery... Highly recommended."
The Wishing Shelf Book Awards

5P1R1T R3V3L4T10N5
Nigel Peace (ISBN 978-1-907203-14-5)

With descriptions of more than a hundred proven prophetic dreams and many more everyday synchronicities, the author shows us that, without doubt, we can know the future and that everyone can receive genuine spiritual guidance for our lives' challenges. World-renowned biologist Dr Rupert Sheldrake has endorsed this book as "...vivid and fascinating... pioneering research..."

A national runner-up in *The People's Book Prize* awards.

THE QUIRKY MEDIUM
Alison Wynne-Ryder (ISBN 978-1-907203-47-3)

Alison is the co-host of the TV show *Rescue Mediums*, in which she puts herself in real danger to free homes of lost and often malicious spirits. Yet she is a most reluctant medium, afraid of ghosts! This is her amazing and often very funny autobiography, taking us behind the scenes of the television production as well as describing how she came to discover the psychic gifts that have brought her an international following.

Winner of the Silver Medal in the national
Wishing Shelf Book Awards.
"Almost impossible to put down."

THE SPIRIT OF THE HEDGEROW
Jo Dunbar (ISBN 978-1-910027-16-5)

The often ignored 'wild weeds' of our hedgerows offer us amazing medicines, delicious food and fascinating legends of human history. The ancient knowledge of our ancestors is brought vividly to life in this beautifully illustrated book by medical herbalist, Jo Dunbar. She shows us the hidden beauty all around us, teaches us what to pick (and to avoid!) and how to use these rich resources, weaving in at the same time the folklore of our natural environment. This book fires the imagination!

Past winner of the Local Legend national
Spiritual Writing Competition
and a Finalist in the *Wishing Shelf Book Awards.*

BROKEN SEA
Nigel Peace (ISBN 978-1-910027-23-3)

In the summer of 1968, at the height of joyful revolution in the West, darker reactionary clouds are gathering elsewhere... Preparing for university, Roy falls helplessly in love for the first time. This is a good thing. Unfortunately, Eva is Czech and her homeland is about to be savagely invaded by the military forces of the Warsaw Pact. This is now a struggle for identity, both personal and national, where neither love nor freedom are tolerated. In the course of one heady and dramatic year, every character in the story will be profoundly changed.

5* *"Packed full of political tension... excellent characterisation and a gripping plot. Highly recommended." The Wishing Shelf Book Awards*

These titles are available as paperbacks and eBooks.
Further details and extracts of these and many other
beautiful books for the Mind, Body and Spirit
may be seen at

www.local-legend.co.uk